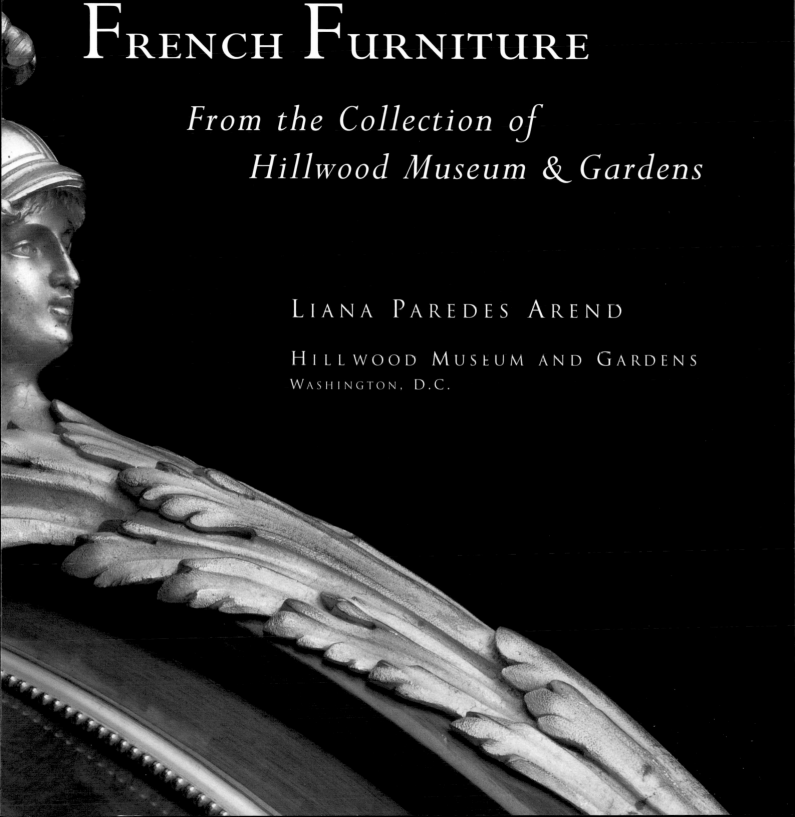

FRENCH FURNITURE

*From the Collection of
Hillwood Museum & Gardens*

LIANA PAREDES AREND

HILLWOOD MUSEUM AND GARDENS
WASHINGTON, D.C.

CONTENTS

FOREWORD 6

MRS. POST, COLLECTOR OF FRENCH FURNITURE 10

INTRODUCTION 22

THE DISTRIBUTION OF SPACES 26
New Thinking for a New Way of Living

LE DERNIER CRI 30
Styles and Fashions during the Ancien Régime

THE CONSUMERS 43
Aristocrats, Financiers, Women, and the Haute Bourgeoisie

THE PRODUCTION SYSTEM 48
Design, the Guilds, and the Luxury Trades
The Role of Architects and Ornamentalists 48
The Guilds 53

MENUISIERIE AND EBÉNISTERIE 60
The Two Main Crafts in Furniture Making
Menuisierie 60
Ebénisterie 77

NOTES 115

SELECTED BIBLIOGRAPHY 118

Foreword

IN THE EARLY TWENTIETH CENTURY, WHEN THE YOUNG POST CEREAL heiress Marjorie Merriweather Post hit her stride as an up-and-coming New York socialite, she realized that it was essential for her self-presentation to become a woman of discerning taste and to create a grand environment that would speak to that taste. Following the newest decorating trend, which aspired to principles of harmonious, classically proportioned interiors, then being fostered by Edith Wharton, Ogden Codman, and Elsie de Wolfe, Marjorie (at the time married to financier E. F. Hutton) set about to assemble one of the most superlative American collections of eighteenth-century French furniture. Sir Joseph Duveen and other noted purveyors of upscale European fine and decorative arts helped train her eye as she purchased a considerable number of pieces to decorate her enormous New York apartment. During the remainder of her life, for this and other homes, including Hillwood, Mrs. Post acquired a remarkable number of outstanding pieces made by the best cabinetmakers of the second half of the eighteenth century. Her collection, though not encyclopedic or highly comprehensive in scope, is extraordinary, if for no other reason than that it was put together by a single person. In this sense, Hillwood's grouping of French furniture is one of the most important in the country; and one that provides an insightful opportunity for research and study. Ever mindful of appropriate settings for her superlative pieces, Mrs. Post insisted that her most official rooms be fitted with lavish period paneling. These magnificent ensembles—providing an undeniably suitable ambiance for her internationally renowned assemblage of imperial Russian and French decorative arts—are vivid expressions of the collecting criteria of one of the most remarkable women collectors of the twentieth century.

I am grateful to Liana Paredes Arend, Hillwood's Acting Deputy Director for Collections and Curator of Western European Art, for this truly informative

publication. She has provided a most useful contextual background to a better comprehension of these magnificent pieces of furniture. Further, I must acknowledge photographer Edward Owen and graphic designer Polly Franchini for their artistic contributions to this beautiful book.

Finally, the staff and I are indebted to the Board of Trustees of the Hillwood Museum & Gardens Foundation for their wholehearted support of the museum's ongoing publishing program. Their enthusiasm and encouragement have inspired us to pursue the highest standards possible for the care and interpretation of, and research into, Mrs. Post's magnificent art collection and estate.

FREDERICK J. FISHER, EXECUTIVE DIRECTOR

Mrs. Post

Collector of French Furniture

*M*ARJORIE MERRIWEATHER POST'S COLLECTION OF FRENCH furniture can be counted among the most important in America assembled by a single person. Mrs. Post began collecting furniture as early as the late 1910s and made purchases continuously in this field until the late 1960s. Marjorie Merriweather Post's genesis as a discerning collector goes back to the second decade of the twentieth century (fig. 2). At that time a young woman of great wealth, married to Edward Close, and a mother of two, Marjorie established some collecting criteria to which she would adhere for the rest of her life. Young Marjorie had grown up in a late Victorian environment where interiors were heavy, busy, and replete with objects that made reference to past historical styles. In those early New York years Marjorie established a personal preference for a completely different aesthetic: that of the arts of late-eighteenth-century France, and of the neoclassical period of Louis XVI in particular, an era when harmony, balance, delicate decoration, superb craftsmanship, and restraint reigned supreme. Two main factors contributed to the shaping of Marjorie's taste in those early years.

One of the turning points in the development of Mrs. Post's taste was the purchase of a grand Manhattan townhouse. In 1919 Marjorie and Edward Close bought a Beaux-Arts mansion originally built in 1907 for the Burden family by Horace Trumbauer, an architect trained at the Ecole des Beaux-Arts in Paris. The lavish building, at the corner of 92nd Street and 5th Avenue was as French on the inside as on the outside. Jules Allard, a French cabinetmaker who had crossed the Atlantic in the late nineteenth century to establish a firm of interior decoration in New York, had been entrusted to design the interiors for the Burden family. Allard's lavish French-style rooms made a tremendous impact on Mrs. Post (fig. 3).

Nobody, however, played a more critical role in Marjorie Merriweather Post's collecting in those early years than Sir Joseph Duveen who "guided her

Fig. 1

MARJORIE
MERRIWEATHER
POST IN
HILLWOOD'S
DRAWING ROOM
ca. 1957
Photography by Horst. ©Vogue.
Condé Nast Publications

Fig. 2
MARJORIE POST
HUTTON AMID
SOME OF HER
FRENCH
FURNISHINGS
New York, ca. 1926

Fig. 3
BURDEN HOUSE
DRAWING ROOM
Jules Allard, decorator
New York, ca. 1916

taste and knowledge," as she would recall years later.[1] Duveen would remain, along with her father, the most influential man in her life. He was the one who introduced her to eighteenth-century France. Duveen put together many study books about the various schools of painting for young Marjorie, surely with the hope of enticing her to buy Old Master paintings from his stock. But despite Duveen's attempts, Marjorie did not develop a passion for Old Masters. Her interests were clearly inclined from the beginning toward the decorative arts, furniture in particular.

The sources from whom she bought furniture could be read as a who's who of art dealers. In the early 1920s Mrs. Post bought several pieces of furniture of great significance from Duveen. Among them is the table attributed to Oeben (fig. 54), which came from the collection of Reverend Sir Philip Grey-Egerton of Oulton Park, and which had been exhibited at the Manchester Art Treasures Exhibition on 1857. The similarly shaped table stamped Roussel (fig. 56) also came from Duveen, and was previously in the collection of Sir Frances Montefiore of Worth Park, Sussex.

The very important Riesener commode (fig. 51), which had originally been in the collection of Lord Hertford (founder of the Wallace Collection) at the Bagatelle, his Parisian house, was a 1931 purchase from Duveen. In 1912, Jacques Seligman had acquired Hertford's collection *'en bloc'* from the heirs of his illegitimate son, Sir Richard Wallace. Seligman then sold this commode to Mrs. Frances Gould, from whom Duveen acquired it.

Unfortunately, two of the most important pieces of furniture acquired from Duveen are not at Hillwood. These were two jewel caskets with Sèvres

Fig. 4
MARJORIE POST
HUTTON DRESSED
AS MARIE
ANTOINETTE
ca. 1926
One of her two porcelain inset
jewelry coffers by Martin Carlin
is in the background.

porcelain plaques by Martin Carlin, one of which can be seen in the background of figure four.

It is evident that initially Mrs. Post carved a niche for herself among the discerning collectors of European works of art mainly through her purchases of furniture and tapestries. One of the jewels of the collection, the Roentgen desk (fig. 5), came to form part of her priceless holdings in 1927. The desk came from Symons, Inc., a firm that a British dealer had established in New York.

Marjorie Merriweather Post's collection grew so much in the first two decades of the twentieth century, that, at the instigation of Duveen, she engaged several authors to prepare a catalogue of her collections to be privately printed. In doing so, she followed most notably in the footsteps of J. P. Morgan, who had undertaken the task of publishing a limited edition of a catalogue of his collections to give out to a selected few. Mrs. Post's position as a collector of furniture was defined in the catalogue's introduction: "Only a collector of discriminating and fastidious taste could have gathered such choice examples of French ébénisterie."[2]

From the mid-1930s to the late 40s Mrs. Post was steadily engaged in collecting decorative arts, but she acquired no significant pieces of furniture during that period. This might be due to the fact that during the second half of the 1930s Mrs. Post was married to Joseph E. Davies, who was at that time serving as U.S. Ambassador in Moscow. She therefore concentrated on collecting Russian art and what was otherwise available in Russia, namely some Sèvres and a few other European works of art, but virtually no furniture.

The last important phase of Mrs. Post's furniture collecting coincides with the purchase of Hillwood in 1955. Her mandate to architect and designers was to refurbish the 1920s neo-Georgian house into a larger, more palatial dwelling that could function both as a home and as a place to showcase her collections. The role of the firm of antique dealers and decorators French &

Fig. 5

*View of roll-top desk in figure
70 showing the mirror that
cranks up from the back.
Swing-out drawers are outfitted
with candleholders and green
silk for protection from the
glare of the candles.*

Co. became critical in those years. The head of the firm, Mitchell Samuels, helped Mrs. Post conceive Hillwood as a museum along the lines of the Jacquemart André and the Nissim de Camondo in Paris and the Huntington and Gardner museums in America.

In those years of decorating Hillwood, French & Co. were in the best position to suggest works of art to complete the interiors. In terms of furniture, French & Co. were the providers of the important suite of chairs and sofas covered in Gobelins tapestry (figs. 35, 36), a gift from Louis XVI and Marie Antoinette to Prince Henry of Prussia. The standing clock by Lieutaud and Berthoud (fig. 13) was a 1956 purchase from the same firm.

McMillen & Co., the other interior design firm involved at Hillwood, also acted as an intermediary with antique dealers to present Mrs. Post with furnishings for purchase. It was through them that Mrs. Post bought the outstanding rococo console tables from Rosenberg & Steibel, one of which is illustrated in figure forty-four. From Dalva Brothers came the lavish desk by Conrad Mauter (fig. 73).

The influence of Mrs. Post's second daughter, Mme. Barzin, on her collecting is especially significant in the area of French furniture. In Paris, her middle daughter avidly pursued great pieces to complete her mother's collection. Among the most outstanding is a swivel chair (fig. 41) that belonged to Marie Antoinette, and a lavish jewelry coffer with cube marquetry (fig. 59). In a letter to her mother the year of this purchase, Mme. Barzin wrote: "I am terribly pleased that you like all the things bought here. About your *coffre à bijoux* . . . it is really a museum piece from every point of view."[3]

In 1958 Mrs. Post hired a curator, Marvin C. Ross (fig. 6). Ross, a Harvard educated art historian, had worked as curator of medieval art at the Brooklyn Museum, as curator of medieval and byzantine art and of decorative arts at the Walters Art Gallery in Baltimore, and as chief curator at the Los Angeles County Museum of Art. Ross extensively researched the furniture

Fig. 6

*Marvin C. Ross, Mrs. Post's
curator, teaching a lesson on
French furniture in Hillwood's
French Drawing Room,
ca. 1958*

Following pages:

*Hillwood's French Drawing
Room*

collection and started to compile notes for a catalogue in this area. As curator
of Mrs. Post's collection, Ross also played a critical role in advising Mrs. Post
on acquisitions.

Despite some differences of opinion between Ross and Mrs. Post, she
collected some great pieces during Ross's tenure as curator. The star addition
was another commode by Riesener, purchased from Duveen Brothers in 1963
(fig. 49). At the time of purchase, and at Mrs. Post's request, Duveen Brothers
sent a lengthy description of the piece and a biography of the cabinetmaker.
Mrs. Post, evidently interested in building up the curatorial files on her
collection, personally wrote back: "This is of course all very useful, but it is
not exactly what I wanted as most of it is quite obvious to any person versed in
beautiful things of this type. What I am after is the history of the commode,
who ordered it and an exact date if possible. I assume the names of the
subsequent owners can be ascertained from the sources in England where you
bought the commode."[4]

All the pieces that Mrs. Post collected so lovingly can be viewed today in
the environment that was created for them at Hillwood. Today, Mrs. Post's
legacy is of special significance. Hillwood's holdings of French furniture can be
counted among the most comprehensive in the country, and are a major source
for this field of study in the Washington area.

Introduction

*T*oward the end of Louis XIV's reign, the French emerged as the undisputed European leaders in the realm of domestic architecture and decorative arts. French élites and architects abandoned the grand and formal style of planning associated with Versailles and turned to the private realm. At the death of the Sun King the aristocrats and high-ranking officers who had lived under a suffocating court etiquette fully freed themselves from the demands of life at Versailles and focused their attention on their Paris dwellings. Together with architects and designers these élites invented a "new art" of domestic design. Soon the reputation of Parisians as the most skillful in the devising of ornaments and in creating the best settings for an extremely pleasant way of life expanded throughout Europe and beyond.

Fig. 7

Detail of Riesener commode,
fig. 49

In the eighteenth century, the private aspects of daily life took on unprecedented importance. In human terms, the Enlightenment quest for what was most individual in man found expression in a greater emphasis on privacy. In architecture, this demand translated into the creation of smaller, private rooms alongside the traditional official rooms. In terms of furniture, eighteenth-century households added new mobile, comfortable, and agreeable furniture to the architectural furniture that constituted the only furnishings of the sixteenth and seventeenth centuries. The relatively "informal" new way of living in intimate surroundings gave rise to an astonishing increase in the variety of furniture shapes. This is perhaps the more important, far-reaching contribution of the eighteenth century to the history of furniture.

Of all the decorative arts, furniture is the one most closely related to architecture. Furniture making was essentially based on architectural concepts and motifs, and was designed to fit within an architectural scheme. The architects, designers of ornament, *marchands-merciers, menuisiers,* and *ébénistes* of

the Ancien Régime outdid themselves in creating new forms of furniture to
adapt to the new spaces. They also excelled in fulfilling—in the most creative
and skillful manner—the demands of an utterly hedonistic society that craved
more functional and comfortable furnishings.

Furniture production, regulated and controlled by the guilds, attained
new levels of technical achievement and sophistication. The principal
manufacturers of furniture were the *menuisiers,* who worked in solid wood and
whose means of decorating surfaces was restricted to carving, and the *ébénistes,*
whose specialty was marquetry and veneers in exotic woods.

THE DISTRIBUTION OF SPACES
New Thinking for a New Way of Living

*P*ERHAPS THE FACTOR THAT MOST INFLUENCED THE CREATION OF furniture in the eighteenth century was the new thinking on the subject of architecture and the distribution of spaces. It is hard for us to grasp the revolutionary thinking that took place in the eighteenth century around the subject of interiors. The words of contemporary Pierre Patte in 1765 most eloquently echoed these changes and their importance: "Nothing has bestowed upon us more honor than the art of the distribution of space in edifices. In the past, we endowed the exterior with all the magnificence. In imitation of the antique and of Italian buildings the interiors were vast but not comfortable . . . the sequence of rooms without a clear connection . . . . One lived for representation, ignoring the art of living with comfort."[5] Indeed if one compares the interiors of Italianate palaces—long enfilades of vast rooms dedicated to ceremonial and official use—with quintessentially French interiors of a century later—smaller private rooms in combination with large ceremonial spaces—one begins to understand the drastic change of thinking around the function and distribution of space.

In the eighteenth century the distribution of rooms underwent critical modifications. Several architects, with Jacques-François Blondel at the forefront, devoted much time and energy to this subject. Blondel, a professor of architecture in Paris, was enormously influential in explaining how to plan and decorate a modern house. The distribution of spaces, he argued, was based on a division between *appartements de parade* (state rooms) and *appartements de commodité* (private rooms). Blondel explained that the *appartements de parade* should be at the front of the house and comprise a vestibule, two antechambers (the first for servants to wait in, the other for people of distinction to gather in), a state bedchamber, a grand reception room, a gallery for displaying the finest works of art, and, of course, a string of salons (figs. 8, 9).

Then there were the *appartements de commodité,* or private living quarters, which consisted of small *cabinets,* studies, and boudoirs (fig. 10). A well-

appointed *appartement* consisted of a bedroom, an anteroom, a study or salon,
and in some cases a bathroom, but as the century progressed dining rooms,
libraries, and boudoirs were added. These rooms were smaller, better heated,
and more agreeable than any private spaces that had been created up to that
time. These were spaces to which one could retreat from public life at a time
when there was an increased desire for a more private, domestic existence.
Private apartments would become essential in an eighteenth-century house
plan. *Appartements de commodité* were also fervently adopted in court circles

Fig. 9

FRENCH DRAWING
ROOM AT
HILLWOOD
East wall
Mid-18th-century paneling
with later additions

where courtiers tried to carry on a private existence on the fringes of official life. In opposition to state rooms, these rooms were apt to receive a less monumental form of decoration.

The development of furniture in the eighteenth century is intimately linked to changes in domestic architecture. An entire array of furniture shapes was created for official and private apartments. This furniture had to accord with the proportions of the room and the magnificence or simplicity of its decoration. Monumental, more architectural types were destined for public spaces. Small-scale, multipurpose furnishings worked better in the private areas of the home.

The arrangement of furniture was likewise subordinated to a room's architecture. Today, when ceremonial schemes of decoration are no longer extant and when informality prevails, it is difficult to envisage the criteria for the arrangement of furnishings of three centuries ago. Furniture scattered about the floor plan—a form to which we are accustomed today—was totally foreign to eighteenth-century sensibilities. In his *Livre d'Architecture* (1745), Germain Boffrand commented that "a room should not resemble a mercer's

Fig. 10
THE LUNCHEON
1739
François Boucher (1703–1770)
Oil on canvas
81 x 65 cm
Courtesy of the Réunion des
Musées Nationaux / Art
Resource, N.Y.

shop."[6] Symmetry and obeisance to the architecture of a room ruled over the furnishings of state rooms. These were mostly filled with console tables and various types of chairs in large quantities arranged against the perimeter of the room. The grand salons of the eighteenth century contained very few pieces of cabinetry. Furniture made by cabinetmakers was found rather in the *petits appartements* (fig. 10). As Bruno Pons remarked, these arrangements were not characteristic of royal or princely mansions, where a certain amount of case furniture was placed.[7]

LE DERNIER CRI

Styles and Fashions during the Ancien Régime

*F*URNITURE MAKERS IN THE PERIOD FROM LOUIS XIV TO THE Revolution appropriated influences from the classical world, from the exotic Far East, and from the recently discovered ruins at Pompeii and Herculaneum, and reworked them into something quintessentially novel and French. The rejection of historicism and the valorization of the new endowed the furniture creations of the period with a special flair.

Although the terms Louis XV and Louis XVI are commonly used to express rococo and neoclassical styles respectively, their reigns actually did not coincide with or trigger the creation of both so-called styles. The rococo was a style that originated with the court but predated the ruler most strongly

associated with it. The "Louis XV" style was, in fact, hegemonic for only some thirty years (1720–1750), beginning with the Regency and ending well before the end of that reign in 1774. The style "Louis XVI" was born approximately twenty years before Louis XVI assumed the throne. And the initiative behind the new aesthetic lay more with the intellectuals and "enlightened" men than with the monarch's sense of how he should be represented.

The years between 1720 and 1760 saw the rococo style unfold, peak, and then subside with the advent of neoclassicism. With Louis XIV's death, courtiers, fully freed from the demands of residence at Versailles, now focused their attention on their Paris dwellings. These places were conceived spatially and decoratively in the new style. Not simply different from the classical style of Versailles associated with Louis XIV at the height of his power, rococo was in many respects its antithesis. In architecture, forms became ethereal and walls lost rigid definitions. A style of unprecedented inventiveness gave free reign to decoration. Ornamentation, which traditionally had played a subordinate role to architecture, became more predominant. Lively sculptural decorations began to cover surfaces (fig. 11). In furniture, rococo favored curved lines, fragile

Fig. 12

*Detail of face and gilt bronze
decorations of the standing
clock in fig. 13*

forms, lightness, elaborate pictorial marquetry, complex veneer work, and highly decorative bronzes.

But when, by the 1740s, the rococo manner became increasingly extravagant and tediously overloaded with meaningless ornament, many advocated a return to a more measured style. Already in 1737, in his *Distribution des maisons de plaisance,* Blondel had criticized rococo's ridiculous jumble of shells, dragons, reeds, and plants. The reaction against the rococo style was not far behind, and in the early 1750s the first manifestations of neoclassicism were appearing in Paris, first in architecture and then in decoration.

The new emerging style was introduced as an antidote to rococo. Neoclassicism, the artistic expression of the Age of Reason, was first embraced by a small group of intellectuals and connoisseurs. In 1749 King Louis XV sent the Marquis de Marigny, brother of Mme. de Pompadour and future *Directeur-général des bâtiments du roi* (a sort of minister of culture), the engraver Charles-Nicholas Cochin, the architect Jacques-Germain Soufflot, and the Abbé Le Blanc to Italy to record the monuments of Antiquity. Upon their return, they advocated a return to classical "good taste" in their well-known "Supplication to silversmiths, sculptors. . . ," which appeared in the *Mercure de France* in December of 1754.

The first expressions of neoclassicism in the decorative arts represented a drastic change of idiom. A standing clock at Hillwood (fig. 13) is an eloquent example of this first radical phase. Its ponderous shape and the rigidity of its bronzes represent not so much the style of neoclassicism adopted by the court but rather the style that was preferred among rich and enlightened art amateurs.

Curves had disappeared. Straight lines were the rule. Neoclassical furniture is characterized by right angles, straight lines, and architectural

Fig. 13

STANDING CLOCK
Case: Balthazar Lieutaud
(d. 1780)
Mechanism: Ferdinand Berthoud
(1727–1807)
Wood marquetry, gilt bronze,
enamel
H. 90 in., W. 19½ in.,
D. 12 in.
16.1

Fig. 14

Detail of sinuous armrest with
classical volutes from dressing-
table chair by Claude Sené,
fig. 41

proportions. The decorative elements that adorn their surfaces were borrowed from Greece and from Rome.

Not everyone, however, adopted this severe style. There was a transition period when a more subdued, tame version of the style was progressively adopted on a larger scale. This "transitional" style was widely accepted for fashionable interiors and furnishings. The "transitional" style proposed a compromise between the frivolity of rococo and the rigorous adaptation of Antiquity. Pieces at Hillwood are mostly in the "transitional style," which is best expressed in its felicitous blending of curves and straight lines. The Sené chair (figs. 14 and 41) is a case in point. Among all furnishings, it was the chair that yielded most reluctantly to the severe precepts of neoclassicism. Chairs with oval backs, softly curved armrests, and generous serpentine outline continued to be made in great numbers.

In their quoting of classical

FIG. 15
COMMODE *"À LA GRECQUE"*
Maker unknown
Paris, ca. 1775
H. 29 in., L. 49 in., D. 27 in.
31.15

FIG. 16

*Detail of side of fall-front desk
in fig. 64 with a marquetry
panel of a trophy of scientific
instruments suspended from a
ribbon.*

Antiquity, the French did not resort to a literal appropriation of decorative elements. Rather, in an enlightened vein, French artists and artisans transcended their historical models and transformed them into new forms with a contemporary flair. If the inspiration from Antiquity was rather serious and solemn in architecture, its adaptation to furniture and decoration was more frivolous. The *"goût grec"* that swept France in the 1760s had in fact very little connection with Ancient Greece. In the widest sense of the word *"goût grec"* was a term of praise vaguely meaning "classical." For all their classical underpinnings, *"goût grec"* or *"à la grecque"* were just catch phrases used commercially by merchants to pin on anything from coffee to hairstyles to snuff boxes. Commodes like the one in figure fifteen were labeled *"à la grecque,"* even if they had nothing to do with Greek furniture. The type became very fashionable. Mme. de Pompadour ordered several for her château at

Ménars (commodes such as this one appear in the inventory taken after her death in 1764).

The popularity of the Antique as a source of design can be measured by the success of the publication of numerous collections of engravings of classical ornament. The classical trophy on the side of the fall-front desk in figure sixteen almost certainly derives from a printed source.[8]

The excavations of Herculaneum and Pompeii and the trips to Italy by art administrators and artists revived interest in the ruins of Antiquity. Painters like Hubert Robert, nicknamed Robert *"des ruines,"* and Gian Paolo Panini created *"capriccios,"* genres of painting in which they arbitrarily gathered several monuments of Antiquity on the same canvas. Their work inspired *marqueteurs* (specialists in marquetry) to transpose these creations onto marquetry panels. The central panel of the Macret commode (fig. 17) features a scene taken from a Panini composition, in which a sybilla preaches among the ruins of the temple of Vesta, the pyramid of Caius Cestius, and the Barberini Vase (fig. 18).[9] Here the *marqueteur* has taken the artistic license of replacing the pyramid with a tree.

After the discoveries of Pompeii and Herculaneum in 1748, greek keys, meanders, egg and dart, and other classical motifs began to decorate surfaces from walls to furniture. Rosettes, acanthus leaves, interlaced ribbons, and strings of pearls appear on borders, friezes, and chair frames.

Another feature of neoclassicism is the treatment of the pastoral subject. Emblems of pastoral life—straw hats, gardening implements, shepherd's staffs—proliferated as decorative motifs (fig. 19). Several architects and designers worked to give full expression to Queen Marie Antoinette's taste for elegant floral decoration.

Fig. 17

*Central panel of commode in
fig. 62, depicting a woman
preaching among classical ruins*

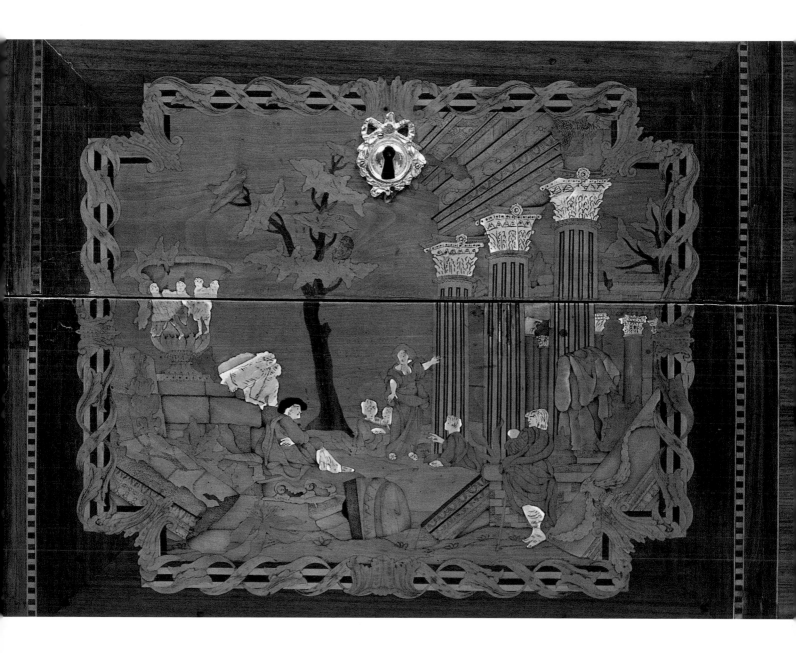

Fig. 18

RUINES À LA PYRAMIDE
Ca. 1750
Gian Paolo Panini
(1691–1765)
Oil on canvas
Courtesy Musée des Beaux Arts,
Valence

Fig. 19
*Central panel of commode in
fig. 49, showing a cluster of
pastoral elements*

THE CONSUMERS

Aristocrats, Financiers, Women, and the Haute Bourgeoisie

ERSAILLES, OPENED TO ANYONE DECENTLY DRESSED—IN OTHER words, wearing a hat and sword—housed a permanent exhibit of the products of France's luxury industries, a "vitrine" that showcased the latest tendencies in interior decoration. From the reign of Louis XIV until the Revolution, Versailles would become a model to follow in matters of building and interior decoration.

Versailles, however, would not provide the only model. The first expressions of other than courtly taste manifested themselves when Versailles was closed during the nine years of the Regency of the Duke of Orléans (1715–1724). After the death of the Sun King and during the minority of this grandson—the future Louis XV—the court dispersed. The center of attention shifted from Versailles to Paris, and Paris began to set the tone in matters of fashion, taste, and decoration. Philippe d'Orléans, a *bon vivant* and passionate collector, resided at the Palais Royal, the new center of influence.

Around him gathered a new kind of high society. The numerous wars of the latter part of the seventeenth century had upset the social order, giving rise to a small group of wealthy entrepreneurs who had profited from warfare and ensuing years of peace. Parisian high society thus no longer consisted of a homogeneous aristocratic elite. In addition to aristocrats it was composed of entrepreneurs, rich bourgeois, financiers who made money speculating in land, farmers-general (a powerful group of tax collectors), parvenus, and fashionable women. This diverse group gravitated towards a "modern" artistic expression, light and youthful like their aspirations. Paris teemed with a brilliant new social life, free of the constraints of stiff court etiquette. Wealthy Parisians became the critical consumers of luxury art. All erected or rebuilt *hôtels,* where the harmony of the decoration and the comfort of the dwellings were a priority.

Such vocations as collecting art and setting up lavish homes became significant elements of self-presentation not only for aristocrats but also for leading financial families and the high robe. In these high-powered fashionable circles the love for the "new" was paramount. Being on the cutting edge of fashion obliged these "fashionistas" to renew their houses and furnishings: "Every six years they change the furnishings. Furniture has become the biggest object of luxury and expense."[10] The old had no intrinsic cultural value; second-hand objects were considered essentially worthless unless they could be remounted to look like something new. In the furniture world, this lack of interest in historicism meant, until late in the eighteenth century, a lack of interest in antique furniture.

Women began to have a more active role in setting fashion. Both Louis XV and his grandson Louis XVI gave their mistresses and wives considerable authority over matters of taste. The feminization of the beautiful trickled down from the Crown to other spheres of power. Mme. de Pompadour, for example, took a central role after mid-century in establishing style. The account books of the merchant Lazare Duvaux, as well as the diary of the *ébéniste* Pierre II Migeon, reveal the vast quantities of money Mme. de Pompadour spent on furnishing her three *châteaux*. Marie Antoinette surrounded herself with fine pieces of jewel-like richness. The silks, porcelains, and furnishings ordered by the queen show her passion for garlands, flowers, ribbons, and tassels.

The inventions of the dressing table, the bedside table, women's writing desks, the *chiffonier,* and many other specifically "feminine" pieces of furniture further reflect women's influence as style makers. *Chiffoniers* (fig. 21) were small, easily portable tables with drawers, in which women kept their sewing and embroidery projects as well as other kinds of *chiffons* or "rags." *Ébénistes* arranged clever drawer mechanisms so that a woman would be spared the necessity of pulling a drawer toward her, a gesture deemed ungainly and inelegant.[11]

The haute bourgeoisie thrived as well under the liberal economic policies of the Regency. They became consumers of luxury art in their attempt to emulate the wealth and prestige of the nobility. However, the bourgeoisie rarely set trends, contenting themselves with following the fashions established by royalty and aristocracy.

With elite society at large making decisions in matters of taste and design, Versailles lost its position as the center of tastemaking in the eighteenth century. Furthermore, fashionable taste at Versailles, although extremely luxurious and refined, was not necessarily *"le dernier cri."* Indeed it could be rather conservative, and sometimes even old-fashioned. Paris frequently had the final word in art and fashion, which reverberated all the way to Versailles.

The Production System

Design, the Guilds, and the Luxury Trades

The Role of Architects and Ornamentalists

*I*N MATTERS OF INTERIOR DECORATION, ARCHITECTS AND DESIGNERS played a decisive role. In the first half of the eighteenth century, architectural treatises offered a compendium of French architecture and interiors.[12] Most of the grand architects of this period (J. H. Mansart, P. Lassurance, J. A. Gabriel, G. Boffrand) were also decorators. These men linked their talents and visions to those of decorators and designers such as G. M. Oppenord, J. A. Meissonier, J. de Lajoue, F. de Cuvillièrs, or N. Pineau who, according to J. F. Blondel, "by means of their experience and skills have improved our dwellings and made them worthy of the opulence of our citizens and of the admiration of unprejudiced nations."[13]

Within the various trades involved in the making of furniture a wide array of design practices was adopted. Design may have been the responsibility of a draughtsman, a master artisan running a large workshop and an extensive system of sub-contraction, an architect, a *marchand-mercier*, or even the client. Attribution of furniture design often remains unresolved for lack of documentary evidence. The existence of a drawing may prove that this was a necessary stage in the preparation of a model, but it is not always possible to use these as the basis for authorship of a design. The so-called "Artois" chairs are a case in point (fig. 25). They may have been the inspiration for the Gobelin covered chair in figure twenty-six, yet the name of the designer remains unknown.

These collaborations are most evident in the coordination of carved wood paneling or *boiseries* with consoles and chairs. Unfortunately not many original ensembles have survived. Of all wall coverings, wood paneling was the preferred form in the eighteenth century. *Boiseries* provided thermal insulation and muted acoustics to a room while enhancing its aesthetic value.

The paneling in the dining room at Hillwood is a prime example of the

Fig. 24

DESIGN FOR A
WALL ELEVATION
WITH WOOD
PANELING

ca. 1720

Attributed to Nicolas Pineau

(1684–1754)

Pen and brown ink, red crayon,
and graphite

234 x 381mm

Cooper Hewitt, National
Design Museum, Smithsonian
Institution

Fig. 25

DESIGN FOR AN
ARMCHAIR

ca. 1776

Anonymous engraving labeled
"à l'Artois" for the younger
brother of Louis XVI, the comte
d'Artois

Musée des arts décoratifs, Paris

Fig. 26

ARMCHAIR FROM
THE PRINCE OF
PRUSSIA SET
Tapestries: Gobelins, Paris,
1784–1786
Wood frame: 19th century
Gilt wood, wool, silk
H. 42 in., W. 29 in., D. 26 in.
31.84

rococo style of the Regency (fig. 23). Representative of a calmer version of the rococo manner that appeared in the second quarter of the eighteenth century, it has some decorative elements that became the leitmotiv of the period. The carving ornamentation relates to the work of Nicolas Pineau (fig. 24). It was Pineau who gave the French interior the character it assumed in the 1730s. His style was widely admired because it adhered to the French late baroque tradition, while enveloping this in fluid ornamentation of great delicacy and inventiveness. Pineau also designed furniture and his style of carved furniture was immensely influential.[14] His designs for relatively small houses, made for somewhat informal lifestyles *("maisons de plaisance"),* epitomize the spirit of French rococo tastes.

Although the work of the architect and designer would be the most evident in a finished house, many more craftsmen were involved. As Sébastien Mercier commented, "When a house is finished, it has not yet been completed; not a quarter of the expenses have been incurred when the *menuisier,* the tapestry worker, the painter, the gilder, the sculptor, the *ébéniste* . . . arrive. The furnishing of an *hôtel* or townhouse takes three more times than its building."[15] Furnishing a house was a great expense indeed and many were ruined in the process.

The Guilds

*T*HE MANUFACTURE OF A PIECE OF FURNITURE WAS A collaborative process as well, one which involved many artists and artisans. The artisans belonged to professional associations, called guilds, that regulated the craft they practiced. Guilds also protected their professional interests such as the right to freedom from commercial competition and the right to litigate. The guild system, established in the Middle Ages, survived until the Revolution.

To understand the furniture-making process it will be helpful to examine how the guilds relating to the furniture industry operated. The two main groups in furniture making were the *ébénisterie* and *menuisierie*. Although lumped together in the same guild, they in fact constituted two separate groups. By *menuisiers* we understand all workers who specialized in furniture made of solid wood. *Ebénistes* specialized in veneered furniture. In addition, there were two other important guilds associated with furniture making: the guild of the casters and chasers—bronze makers, who supplied mounts for the furniture (fig. 27)—and that of upholsterers. These groups functioned as subsidiaries to the *menuisiers* and *ébénistes,* working under their instruction. Therefore the *ébéniste* and the *menuisier* were the ones who stamped—by entitlement as well as by obligation—a piece of furniture.

In order to become a master in any of these guilds, a long specialization process was required. Apprenticeship was the norm of artisanal training in the furniture trades. To get started in the trade, a child would enter a workshop in early adolescence. His apprenticeship lasted from five to seven years, during which time the parents often paid the master sums for their son's maintenance and support. After this training period, the apprentice would emerge as a

Fig. 27

Bronze rail from roll-top desk in fig. 73

The work of a skilled caster and gilder

competent journeyman and could start receiving payment for his services. After this, the assistant would be fully qualified to become a master in his guild. But often times he would have to wait longer because no vacancy existed or because he could not afford the fees, which were quite high at the time. On average, no more than 400 practitioners could operate as cabinetmakers in Paris at the same time. Once a master, he could open a shop and take assistants and apprentices.

A quicker way to secure a mastership was to marry a master's widow. The widow of a deceased master was entitled to keep his workshop if she had qualified journeymen working in it. For many assistants the opportunity of marrying the master's widow and taking over an established workshop was a chance not to be missed. Jean-François Oeben married the daughter of François Vandercruse, known as "Lacroix," maker of the fall-front desk in figure forty-eight, and in this manner he eventually inherited his workshop.

Despite the power of the guilds, not every furniture craftsman conformed to guild practices. Many practiced on the fringes, away from the constraints of guild regulations. There were free craftsmen or *artisans libres* whose work tended to be of inferior quality. They nevertheless caused irritation to the masters because of their competition in the market and their low prices. Also operating in the margins were a group of privileged artisans, who, under the auspices of the crown, worked in an environment free from guild regulations. The Louvre, the Arsenal, and the Gobelins were the major centers of employment for these craftsmen.

As a result of the rivalries between certain free craftsmen and guild members, regulations were introduced in 1743 to compel every master to possess an iron stamp with which to strike his name onto his pieces of furniture (fig. 28). The stamp is one of the most important factors in identifying authorship in French furniture, but it can also be misleading. It could be easily faked. Or it could fail to indicate authorship, as we shall see.

Fig. 29
SMALL ROUND
TABLE (*guéridon*)
Paris, ca. 1770
Pierre Migeon III (active
1761–1775)
Wood marquetry, gilt bronze,
brass
H. 31 in., D. 14 in.
31.24

The second stamp we find in French eighteenth-century furniture is that issued by the *Jurande* (Wardenship). This committee was responsible for enforcing guild rules and controlling the quality of furniture. The wardens made periodic visits to shops and stamped every piece meeting with their approval. The *juré's* mark reads *JME,* which stands for *Jurande des menuisiers et ébénistes.*

Despite the regulations, stamps are not frequently found on genuine pieces of French eighteenth century furniture. There are several explanations for their absence. Some artisans may not have marked pieces because of resentment of the rule, and others because of negligence. There were also those privileged artisans working for the Crown who were exempt from using it.

It is even more complicated to discern in which capacity a craftsman may have stamped a piece of furniture. Some cabinetmakers were also dealers, and in many instances they stamped the pieces they sold in their capacity as traders. This was the option preferred by the more successful—or more enterprising—craftsmen. It involved more risks and a different system of production. The master's stamp would be used in pieces leaving his shop, though this in no way guaranteed that he had in fact manufactured it. A *marchand-mercier,* or trader in decorative objects, employed other masters and limited his intervention to the final stage of production when he placed his stamp on the finished article to attest to its quality. These *merciers* differed from the mainstream *mercier* in that they had some involvement in production. Pierre Migeon, for example, was an *ébéniste* of the Faubourg who specialized in the manufacture of mechanical furniture for a wide range of uses (fig. 29). He later worked by royal appointment and his business grew to such an extent that he then tried his hand at trade. We know that at some point he had at least seven master *ébénistes,* two master varnishers, three master *menuisiers,* two carvers, five casters, and four gilders in his employ. It is difficult to ascertain whether he signed the tambour table in figure twenty-eight in his capacity as dealer or as cabinetmaker.

Some craftsmen tried not to use a stamp because they sold through a dealer who preferred craftsmen's anonymity. This was not unusual. Some masters deliberately sought to place themselves under a dealer, finding it increasingly difficult to survive by the procurement of direct commissions alone. The *ébéniste* Martin Carlin was an extremely talented craftsman who preferred to supply the leading merciers, thereby ensuring a regular, if modest, income. The volume of orders he received forced him to move to larger premises, down the road from the humble workshop in rue Saint-Antoine where he had started out as an *ébéniste*. It was named *Au Saint Esprit* and was housed in an old building, and comprised five rooms, three of which served as workshops and showcases. He remained there until he died in 1785. Unusually for an *ébéniste*, he left no debts, thus leaving his wife and three children on a firm financial footing.[16] The table in figure thirty expresses the inventiveness and delicacy of his creations.

Fig. 30
TWO-TIERED
CONSOLE TABLE
Paris, ca. 1775
Martin Carlin (active
1766–1785)
Wood, marble, gilt bronze,
lacquer
H. 29 in.,W. 31 in., D. 15 in.
31.28

Fig. 31
LADY'S WRITING
TABLE
Paris, ca 1785–1793
Table: Nicolas Lannuier (active
1783–1804)
Porcelain plaques: Sèvres
Wood marquetry, gilt bronze,
porcelain
H. 30 in., W. 26 in., D. 18 in.
31.25

And then, of course, there was the guild of the *marchand-merciers*, "sellers of everything, makers of nothing," as the *Encyclopédie* called these fashionable dealers in decorative objects. They may not have made anything by hand themselves—they were in fact strictly forbidden to do so—but they certainly had a hand in giving directions to craftsmen who would then execute pieces accordingly. The practice of inlaying furniture with Chinese and Japanese lacquer owes much to the inventiveness of the *marchand-merciers*, as does the custom of decorating furniture with porcelain plaques. Two *marchand-merciers* had a virtual monopoly on obtaining such plaques from the Sèvres factory: Simon-Philippe Poirer and Dominique Daguerre. Martin Carlin was one of the markers who specialized in such practices and most certainly is the *ébéniste* behind the table on figure thirty-one, despite the fact that it bears the stamp of Charles Nicolas Lannuier. There are obvious signs of alteration of what originally must have been a *jardinière* or planter by Carlin into a table by Lannuier. The Sèvres plaques with blue celeste borders and scattered sprays of roses have paper stickers on their backs showing the crossed L's—the royal cypher used as the factory's mark—and a price in ink.

Menuisierie and Ebénisterie

The Two Main Crafts in Furniture Making

*T*hese two crafts existed side by side in the same guild in eighteenth-century Paris, but the distinctions between the two practices ran very deep. From the time of Louis XIV, craftsmen who worked in ebony (hence the name *ébénistes*) were differentiated from those who worked on chairs or on furniture of solid wood. *Ébénistes* excelled and specialized in the technique of veneering.

Menuisierie

The corporation of menuisiers or joiners' guild, encompassed several specialties, including *carrossiers* or coach builders, and *menuisiers* or carpenters. These *menuisiers* consisted of two types. First, those makers of architectural woodwork such as paneling (fig. 32), doors, and console tables, and second, makers of movable woodwork, or furniture, such as most chairs, beds and screens, some consoles, and mirror and picture frames. Almost all *menuisiers* were French, and many belonged to dynasties of chair makers like the Tilliard the Sené and the Jacob families.

Fig. 32

Detail of carved paneling, ca. 1730, in Hillwood's dining room, the work of a menuisier en bâtiment, *maker of architectural woodwork*

Seat furniture was the principal output of *menuisier* workshops. This category of furniture was the one most closely associated with rank as well as with architecture and interior design.

The armchair, the chair, and the folding stool had been at the center of political life and of court intrigues. At Versailles, the king and queen sat on armchairs, the prince and princesses of the blood on chairs, and duchesses on folding stools. All other members of the court had to stand before the royal couple. Saint-Simon's *Mémoires* bristle with scandalous anecdotes over seating arrangements during the reign of the Sun King. Folding stools *(pliants)* were intimately linked to the norms of court etiquette. Folding stools were ever-present in the *appartements de parade* in royal residences and other houses of

distinction, and were always arranged along the walls of a room. The Hillwood *pliants* (fig. 33) may have been part of a set made for Versailles or another royal residence. In the official portrait of Louis XV by Carle Van Loo, the king stands next to a stool whose struts are remarkably similar to those of Hillwood's *pliants*.[17]

The relation of furniture to architecture is clearly evidenced in how chairs were categorized depending upon their placement in a room. In the eighteenth century there were two types of chairs, each distinguished by its function and position within a room. These were the *meublants* (or fixed furniture) and the *courants* (circulating furniture), which developed according to the evolution of the Parisian *appartement*. The *chaises courants* possessed an intimate quality which the *meublants*, destined for reception rooms, assemblies of state, and salons, did not. The *meublants* were frequently designed by the architect himself, and their decoration often recalls that of *boiserie* (wall paneling). The *chaise courant* was usually intended for less formal rooms.

The suite of chairs with Beauvais tapestry covers depicting scenes from La Fontaine's fables (fig. 34) belongs to the category of *chaises meublants*. Of the type known as *"à la reine"*—that is with cabriole legs and straight backs—they were meant to be set against the wall. The armrests, which in the baroque period had been the vertical prolongation of the front legs, were set back by a quarter length of the side rails. This change was triggered by the fashion of paniers or hoop skirts, which François Boucher, in his *Histoire du Costume*, dates to approximately 1715. The costume of the day consisted of full dresses with hoop skirts and more than three and a half meters of silk and brocade. Although there are chairs in existence, dating from 1680 to 1690, that already display set-back armrests, it did not become the general standard until the period from 1720 to 1730 and it lasted until 1768 or 1770.[18] In the eighteenth century, tapestry manufacturers tried to diversify their production by making less monumental works. Both Gobelins and Beauvais found tapestry covers to

be a commercial success. During the reign of Louis XV, Beauvais made several suites of tapestry for covering furniture. The Hillwood suite is covered with animal vignettes representing La Fontaine's fables, based upon designs by Jean-Baptiste Oudry, one of the principal designers at the factory from 1726 and its codirector from 1734.

If Beauvais covers were relatively numerous, Gobelins covers were by

Fig. 34

PAIR OF
ARMCHAIRS
(fauteuils à la reine)
Paris, ca. 1760
Walnut, tapestry. Covered with
Aubusson tapestries depicting
scenes from La Fontaine's fables
Each H. 37 in.,W. 25 in.,
D. 22 in.
31.62; 31.63

Fig. 35
ARMCHAIR
Tapestries: Gobelins, Paris,
1784–1786
Wood frame: 19th century
Gilt wood, wool, silk
H. 42 in., W. 29 in., D. 26 in.
31.82

Fig. 36

*Detail of canapé from the
Prince of Prussia set showing a
close-up of the Gobelin tapestry
seat*

contrast exceptional. The tapestries of the chairs in figures twenty-five and thirty-six were ordered by Louis XVI and Marie Antoinette in 1784. They were included in a generous gift to Prince Henry of Prussia, brother of Frederick the Great, when he visited Paris in 1784. The gift was part of the Crown's concerted effort to foster French luxury industries by presenting their products as diplomatic gifts. It was Louis Tessier, a noted flower painter, who contributed the floral compositions to be woven for this suite at the Gobelins' factory. The Gobelins worked mostly for the Crown whereas Beauvais took private commissions as well.

Although the frames of this suite may be nineteenth century, they must have replicated the originals, at least in outline, since the tapestries conform perfectly to the frames. Oval-shaped backs appear to have been developed from the mid-1760s as confirmed by a Badouin gouache of 1765.[19] In 1758, Maurice Jacques, a painter from the Manufacture de Gobelins, submitted designs for a set of draperies decorated with oval medallions after paintings by François Boucher. The project was apparently based on an idea by J. G. Soufflot, the director of the Gobelins, and was first ordered in 1763 for Croome Court, the residence of Lord Coventry. From 1768 or 1769, *chaises à la médallion* were also produced to complement these wall hangings, which presently reside in the Metropolitan Museum of Art in New York. As mentioned in the previous chapter, this chair model was labeled "à l'Artois" for the comte D'Artois, younger brother of Louis XVI.

Tapestry (fig. 36) has been better preserved than other types of upholstery. Despite the fact that very little of the upholsterer's work has survived the ravages of time, the relevance of the *tapissiers* in matters of decoration was critical. It was to the upholsterer that the client would

Fig. 37
Detail of folding stool (pliant),
fig. 33

normally go to order chairs.
Besides, the work of the
upholsterer was the most visible
in a finished household.
Increasingly, upholsterers were
employed to oversee the work of
other tradesmen, and on many
occasions they were given charge
of whole decorative schemes.
This intrusion in areas normally
reserved for architects provoked
constant friction between the
two professions.

Among the upholsterer's inventions one could cite upholstering "*à châssis.*"
Used on seat furniture—and on Hillwood's Gobelin suite—the upholstery is
stretched across separate frames that are removable from the chair by turn
buttons or screws. This method, introduced between 1725 and 30, is
synonymous with chairs of the highest quality and was used only for extremely
wealthy clients. Upholstery "*à châssis*" was easily changeable according to the
seasons: silk for the summers, and usually velvet or needlepoint for the
winters. It was not uncommon in wealthy households to have a valet in charge
of the preservation and seasonal changes of upholstery.

Both Hillwood suites were completed with canapés and sofas. Inspired by
the divans used in the Ottoman empire, these could comfortably accommodate
various guests at a time and avoided the need to bring more chairs from
another room. About these new forms Voltaire, a witness of the fashions of his
time, made the following comment: "nowadays, the customs are simpler and
ladies use canapés and chaises longues without disconcerting society."[20]

The role of a *menuisier* varied according to how elaborate the carving of a

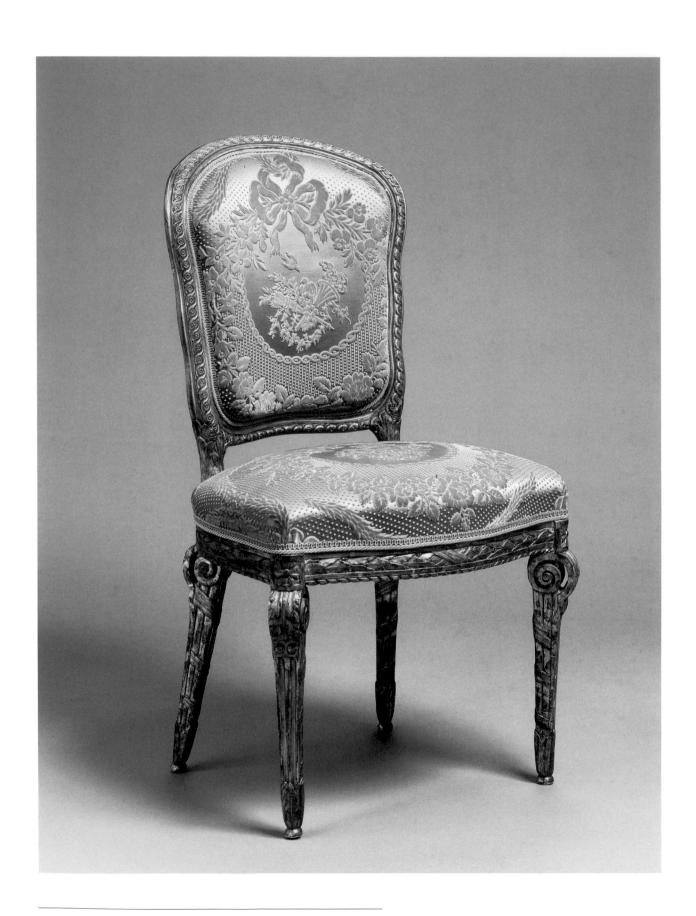

Fig. 38
CHAIR
Paris, ca. 1770
Georges Jacob (1739–1814)
Gilt wood, silk
H. 35 in.,W. 19 in., D. 18 in.
34.94.1

chair was to be. *Menuisiers* were able to execute simple carving, but when something finer was required, they would subcontract the work to the *sculpteur*. The painting and gilding of chairs was the specialty of the *peintres-doreurs* who worked not for the chair maker but for the *marchand-tapissier* or upholsterer (fig. 37).

The suite of chairs and two sofas stamped by Georges Jacob (fig. 38) have very elaborate carving, surely the work of a skilled wood carver. What is most notable, aside from the crisp quality of the carving and the lightness of the design, is the extremely refined use of two tones of gold—yellow and green *("citron")*—in the gilding (fig. 39). The ribbon carved around the chair's legs is gilded green-gold, as are the laurel leaves of the seat frame. Stylistically, this suite is "transitional" in character, with soft, curving lines reminiscent of rococo combined with decorative motifs that bespeak neoclassicism. In type they belong to the category of circulating chairs *(courants)* generally to be found in small rooms or added as a supplement to larger rooms. Georges Jacob was the founder of one of the most important and long-lasting dynasties of chair makers. Jacob arrived in Paris at a young age. In the last years of the Ancien Régime, he benefited from the commissions of the *Garde Meuble*.[21] His talent and the stylishness of his compositions attracted the attention of Marie Antoinette, for whom anything novel was always a source of interest. He produced a considerable quantity of *à l'antique* pieces for the queen, including furniture for her apartments at Saint Cloud. At the same time, his shop was frequented by the haute bourgeoisie, artists, and intellectuals, among whom circulated ideas which would soon break out in Revolution, and which Jacob himself would support.

Many chairs had a specific function. From the Regency onward, the *salons de compagnie* and the *appartements de commodité* began to be filled with lighter and more comfortable chairs. The curiously low chairs known as *chauffeuses* (fig. 40) were another delightful creation of the period. Low fireside chairs

Fig. 39
Detail of fig. 38

belonged in the private apartments of a home, and in bedrooms and boudoirs in particular.

The dressing-table chair is an eighteenth-century creation (fig. 41). The low back and swivel seat would have facilitated the powdering of hair. The maker of this chair, Claude I Sené, was a member of an important Parisian family of *menuisiers* who worked on a regular basis for the Crown. The stamp of the *Garde Meuble de la Reine* branded on the bottom of the seat indicates that the chair was part of the personal furniture created for Queen Marie Antoinette (fig. 42). In 1784, King Louis XVI acquired Saint Cloud from the Orléans family and made it a personal property of the queen, a place for her to spend summers with the children. In the same year, her personal *Garde Meuble* was created. Jean-Baptiste Sené (master in 1769) was the principal supplier of furniture to the queen from 1785 to 1791, a period which she devoted to the decoration of Saint-Cloud. It has been speculated that this chair could have been made for the queen's *cabinet de toilette* at Saint-Cloud.

During the neoclassical period, chairs with straight legs and oval or rectangular backs were made in great numbers, but those with cabriole legs continued to be in favor for a long time as well. Louis XV, faithful to the sinuous lines of his youth, did not possess a chair or armchair with straight legs, whereas his grandson, despite embracing straight lines for legs, always preferred chairs with rounded corners as a result of his myopia (fig. 43).

Chairs were not the only output of *menuisiers* workshops. Beds, fire screens, and console tables were also their specialty. The term console was taken from architectural vocabulary. Indeed it was one of the most architectural shapes of furniture, one that architects often delighted in designing. Consoles were the work of the *menuisiers en bâtiment* who also executed the *boiseries* in accordance with the architect's designs. Such tables were favorite vehicles of expression for wood sculptors who carved their

Fig. 40

LOW CHAIRS
(chauffeuses)
Beaune (France), ca. 1750
Jean-Vincent Montfort
Gilded walnut, silk
H. 20 in.,W. 23 in.
31.86, 31.87

Fig. 41

SWIVEL CHAIR

Paris, ca. 1785

Claude I Sené (1724–1792)

Gilt wood, leather

Branded with inventory number

467

H. 30 in.,W. 26 in., D. 22 in.

31.85

Fig. 42

Mark of Garde Meuble de la Reine *on bottom of chair seat, detail of fig. 41*

Fig. 43
ARMCHAIR
Paris, ca. 1780
Nicolas Denis Delaisement
(became a master in 1776)
Gilt wood, silk
H. 36 in., W. 24 in., D. 20¾ in.
31.90.1

Fig. 44

CONSOLE TABLE

Paris, ca. 1730

Gilt oak, marble

H. 32 in.,W. 50 in., D. 24 in.

31.54

Fig. 45

CONSOLE TABLE
Paris, ca. 1785
Gilt wood, marble
H. 33 in., W. 51 in., D. 23 in.
31.56

surfaces with exuberant ornamentation. The console in figure forty-four is a great example of the energetic design, amazing plasticity, and vigorous spiraling movement of the best of rococo design. The term table *en console* or, in the abbreviated form, *console* consisted of two carved legs, normally curving inwards, supporting a heavy marble top.

Later, *consoles* became unfashionable, but the word continued to be employed for a table and supports, usually of semicircular design, and most frequently with four or six legs connected by a stretcher (fig. 45). Instead of the curvaceous outline of the rococo example, this table has a softly curving profile. The rectilinear, tapering, fluted legs are highly architectural in form. The scrolling vine, the square rosettes, and bold swag ornamentation are all part of the repertoire of the *"goût antique."*

Eбénisterie

Eбénistes specialized in applying veneers to a solid core of wood. Original to Germany and the Low Countries, this technique of applying precious woods onto a layer of a more common solid wood, or "carcass" was not a French novelty. However, the art of marquetry was brought to new heights in France in the seventeenth and eighteenth centuries. *Ebénistes* were concentrated in the Faubourg Saint-Antoine, east of the Bastille. This was not a fashionable quarter, and most of the clientele did not care to visit the area to shop for furniture. Therefore, most *ébénistes* sold through a middleman, often a *marchand-ébéniste*, the name given to those cabinetmakers who had shops selling to the public.

In contrast with the make-up of the *menuisiers*, many of the *ébénistes* were foreign, or of foreign origin. Several came

Fig. 46

Detail of floral marquetry panel in Riesener commode shown in fig. 49

Fig. 47
    Open view of Fig. 48

from the Low Countries and various areas of what is today Germany. It was in the southern part of the Low Countries that the naturalist floral marquetry first appeared around 1655. Enhanced with tortoise shell, ivory, and stains it became a celebrated form of cabinetry during the reign of Louis XIV.

The main aim of early eighteenth-century marquetry was to imitate painting. Marquetry woods were stained blue, yellow, red, green, brown, black, and grey to achieve more pictorial effects. Sadly, these stains, which must have endowed furniture with extraordinary polychromatic effects, appear dull and faint today because of their exposure to light and the effect of varnishes. Only in places that were not exposed much to sun can one appreciate the brilliance of their original tints. Such is the case of the interior of the fall-front secretary by Roger Van der Cruse, also known as "Lacroix," (figs. 47 and 48) where the green stain on the pattern of stripes is still very vivid.

The indisputable master of pictorial marquetry in the eighteenth century was Jean-François Oeben. The panel at the front of the commode in figure fifty-one is certainly one of his models, in this case executed by his most celebrated pupil Jean-Henri Riesener. As an apprentice to Oeben, Riesener mastered the techniques for crafting pictorial marquetry. The realistically rendered basket of flowers reveals all the refinements and naturalism learned from his master.

The commode was the work of *ébéniste*rie par excellence. An invention of the early eighteenth century, commodes appear to have replaced the coffers where linens and night robes were kept. Thus, in the beginning, commodes were used more often in bedrooms than in any other room. The commode was heavy and rested on short legs so that it looked like an old-fashioned chest, yet it was a "chest of drawers," a far more convenient piece of furniture to use than the chest had been. The fact that it was *"plus commode"* (more convenient) than an old-fashioned chest, gave it its French name. The name took some time to catch on. Writing a letter about presents given at court in 1718, the Duchesse

d'Orléans thus felt constrained to explain to a friend that "a commode is a big table with big drawers [and] beautiful decorations."[22]

Despite their functional aspect, commodes were to a large extent ornamental features of rooms, taking the place of pier tables. An object that so combined beauty and function was irresistible when introduced. The large front face of commodes offered a splendid surface for decoration, and the opportunity was soon seized upon, to great effect.

Jean-Henri Riesener is the maker of the two most outstanding commodes at Hillwood (figs. 49 and 51). In 1774, the year in which Louis XV died and his grandson became king, Riesener was appointed *ébéniste du roi,* replacing the elderly Gilles Joubert. For the next ten years, Riesener, a cabinetmaker of German descent, enjoyed the full favor of the court, supplying more than 700 pieces of furniture for extravagant sums.

The commode in figure forty-nine is of the same design as the one delivered to Louis XVI's bedchamber at Versailles and now at Windsor Castle. This monumental commode has a bulging center with two drawers, flanked by

Fig. 48

FALL-FRONT
SECRETARY *(secretaire à abbatant)*
Paris, ca. 1780–1790
Attributed to Roger Van der Cruse, also known as "Lacroix"
Wood marquetry, gilt bronze, porcelain, H. 51 in.,
W. 33¾ in., D. 13½ in.
31.4

Fig. 49

COMMODE
Paris, ca. 1775
Jean-Henri Riesener
(1734–1806)
Wood marquetry, gilt bronze, marble
H. 38 in., W. 67 in., D. 26 in.
31.11

two concave panels concealing cupboard doors. One turn of the key simultaneously unlocks the two large drawers and springs open the side doors. The central panel with a pastoral still life of a basket of flowers, a sheaf of wheat with a sickle, a straw hat, a tambourine, and a pair of turtledoves reflects the love of the outdoors that became fashionable in aristocratic circles. The side panels feature urns of burl-wood veneer, in imitation of jasper, filled with cascading floral arrangements far removed from the more simple floral marquetry seen in more pedestrian pieces of furniture. The Hercules mask mounted at the center of the top frieze, the lion's paws, and the winged mask at the bottom (fig. 50) convey a sense of heroic virtue and strength that would have been suitable in the chambers of a high-ranking member of court or of the royal family.

The peculiar arrangement of the front as a façade with seemingly superimposed decorative elements is repeated on the second Riesener commode in figure fifty-one that is of a slightly later date. This one, of more decisively neoclassical shape with a rectilinear outline, is decorated with a realistically rendered basket of flowers flanked by two panels of jasper vases laden with flowers similar to those on the commode in figure forty-nine. Classical busts—also known to have been used by Martin Carlin—decorate and protect the corners. A variant of the winged mask adorns the center of the apron. The sides of both pieces are veneered with finely executed trellis marquetry enclosing a rosette (fig. 52). Each diamond shape is banded with strips of amaranth edged with extremely thin filets or bands of lighter wood. The restrained treatment of the less important elements evidences the hand of the great master.

At the beginning of the eighteenth century, case furniture was principally intended for use in small, intimate rooms, but gradually found its way into the more public areas of a house. The large number of small pieces of furniture created in the eighteenth century leads to the conclusion that the more refined

Fig. 50

*Detail of bronze mount at the
bottom center of commode in
fig. 49, showing a male winged
and masked figure*

Fig. 51

COMMODE
*Paris, ca. 1775–1780
Jean-Henri Riesener
(1734–1806)
Wood marquetry, gilt bronze,
marble
H. 35 in., W. 56 in., D. 22 in.
31.10*

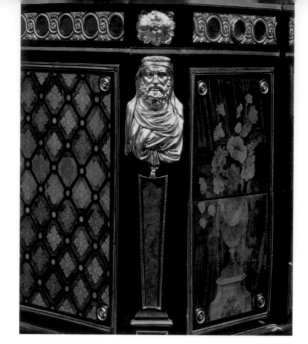

the society became, the more its furnishings responded to increasingly specific demands. Some pieces were ingeniously designed to serve more than one purpose. Some were even light enough to be carried from room to room.

This is the case of the dressing table, of which Hillwood has two examples (figs. 54 and 56). Both have sliding tops that when pushed backward reveal a drawer fitted with several small drawers as well as compartments for creams and cosmetic pots. The central part could be used for either reading or writing. The central panel is hinged at the front and can be raised and turned by means of a hidden ratchet. The writing surface can be inverted to show the mirror on the other side (fig. 53).

The table with the floral marquetry (fig. 54), although stamped Boichod, is more likely the work of Jean-François Oeben, for various reasons. Although Pierre Boichod was an artisan *privilegié du roi* (a privileged cabinetmaker working for the Crown), the core of his oeuvre seems to be rather unambitious. Therefore this piece would seem anomalous for his kind of work. It is possible, however, that his stamp appears on it rather as the restorer's than the maker's. Stylistically, the table relates to the signed and attributed works of Jean-François Oeben and hence should be attributed to him. The delicate rendering of the floral marquetry, partitioned by ribbon bands on the top, is in line with Oeben's skills (fig. 55). The trophies at the center and on the right side of the table are decorated with symbols of rustic life. The one on the left is an emblem of war, whereas the one on the top is a hunting trophy. All allude to a personality of great fortitude and valor as well as of great sensibility and appreciation of the natural world. The hunting trophy links the table with an aristocrat since this was the only group to have the privilege of the hunt during

Fig. 53
LADY'S WRITING
AND DRESSING
TABLE
View of open table, fig. 54

Fig. 54

LADY'S WRITING
AND DRESSING
TABLE
Paris, ca. 1760. Attributed to
Jean-François Oeben (active
1751–1763).
Wood marquetry, gilt bronze
Table stamped Boichod under
front rail. H. 28 in., W. 31 in.,
D. 14 in. 31.23

Fig. 55
Top view, fig. 54

Fig. 56

Fig. 57
LADY'S WRITING
AND DRESSING
TABLE
Paris, ca. 1770
Pierre Roussel (1723-1782)
Wood marquetry, gilt bronze,
ivory, mother of pearl
H. 29 in.,W. 30 in., D. 17 in.
31.30

the Ancien Régime. Oeben is known to have made several mechanical tables such as this one. Sophisticated mechanisms such as drawers opening with one turn of the key and the top sliding back were his specialty, one that was eagerly adopted by other colleagues.

By contrast the quality of the marquetry on the table in figures fifty-six and fifty-seven seems more naïve. The top (fig. 57) shows a lively harbor scene. Stains, ivory, mother of pearl, and different types of carving have been used to create a pictorial effect. Similar pictures in marquetry can be seen on related pieces signed by other *ébéniste*s. Such repetitions of analogous scenes suggest that they must have come from the same source, namely *marqueteurs,* or specialists in veneered pictures, who supplied multiple *ébéniste*s. Pierre Roussel, whose stamp appears on the bottom of this table, was one of those makers turned dealers.

Naïve marquetry can also be seen in a pair of *encoignures* or corner cabinets in figure fifty-eight. To comply with the indispensable symmetry of eighteenth-century arrangements, *encoignures* usually came in pairs. The Hillwood examples are decorated with a still life, framed by a curtain, showing a desk *(bureau plat)* on which stand a smaller writing desk, inkstand, a letter, a sheet of paper, a book, and two floral ornaments. The marquetry lacks sophistication and fits into the category of naively rendered pictures among which one can also cite a whole group of furnishings decorated with Chinese objects (fig. 68).

Geometric designs were among the later developments in the patterns of marquetry. The jewel chest in figure fifty-nine is covered with cubes, rendered by color stains, that create an illusion of three-dimensionality. This form of chest on a stand was derived from Renaissance marriage coffers in which a bride kept her trousseau. By the late seventeenth century, these had been reduced in size to hold jewels, small valuables, or toiletry items. This one with plain veneer interiors (fig. 60) and lavish marquetry and bronzes was in all likelihood used to hold jewels and other such valuables. Hillwood's coffer (fig. 59) reflects the strong influence of Oeben's work, the king of cube marquetry and *ébéniste méchanicien* par excellence. The coffer bears little resemblance to other comparable ones. It is larger than most. Its mounts are also unlike any others on French furniture from that period. The asymmetrical floral escutcheon that decorates the front, the mermaid and merman astride a dolphin at the front of the table, the elaborate scrolled hinges on the back all have no parallel with other mounts of the period (fig. 61). The combination of rococo mounts and geometric marquetry is surprising. Stylistically, it could be explained either by the piece's transitional character or by the owner's particular preferences.

As aforementioned, *ébénistes* were strictly forbidden to make their own mounts. For these, they had to go to one of two separate guilds: the *fondeurs-ciseleurs* or the *ciseleurs-doreurs*.

The decorative form of mounts is inseparable from their function. They

Fig. 58
PAIR OF CORNER
CABINETS *(Encoignures)*
Paris, ca. 1785
Wood marquetry, gilt bronze,
marble
H. 36¼ in., W. 25 in.,
D. 15¼ in.
31.19; 31.20

FRENCH FURNITURE IN THE HILLWOOD COLLECTION

Fig. 59
JEWELRY CHEST
(*Coffre de Bijoux à Voyage*)
Paris, ca. 1760
Wood marquetry, gilt bronze
H. 40 in.,W. 25 in., D. 19 in.
31.27

emphasized the line of the piece and often provided protection for its vulnerable edges and surfaces. The finest examples were fire-gilt with mercury. But there were also simple brass mounts that were left ungilded. A bronze began as a drawing, which a sculptor then translated into wax for casting. Because of the expense of the design process, molds were reused and bronze designs became standardized. The commercial distribution of certain standard types explains why the same mounts appear in the work of different cabinetmakers. A case in point is provided by the mounts on the *encoignures* (fig. 58), which are identical to the ones on the Macret commode (fig. 62).

Some mounts used by top cabinetmakers have a recognizably individual character. For example, branches of acorns tied at the bottom and flanking a central plant as seen in figure sixty-three recur in the work of Martin Carlin.

Most mounts were attached to the wood with highly visible steel-headed screws that contrasted oddly with the careful gilding and chasing of the mounts themselves. This demonstrates the disaffection of common laborers and the differing concerns of each guild. King's cabinetmakers such as Oeben and Riesener were granted the right to employ their own bronze casters, chasers, and gilders. It was they who first thought to conceal the screws of mounts by concealing them with a decorative feature. Later, Riesener dispensed with screws altogether, attaching many of his mounts by screwing short threaded rods at the back of each mount. These in turn passed through holes in the woodwork and were secured by nuts inside the framework (see figs. 50, 52).

Despite some general repetition of models, bronze makers also fabricated some outstanding examples of great sculptural value. Such is the case of the mount at the center of the roll-top desk in figure seventy-three, which depicts a putto reclining against a truncated column (fig. 64).

Bronze mounts were almost always subcontracted. Although this practice was not as widespread for marquetry panels, there is evidence that that marquetry could also be subcontracted. There were some specialists in this

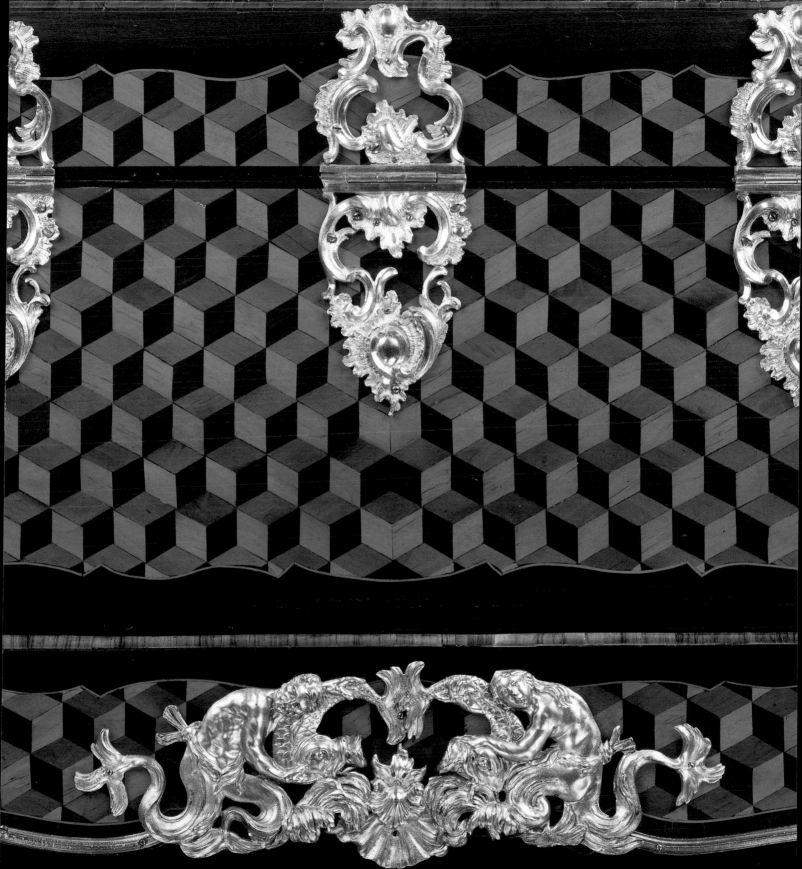

Fig. 62

COMMODE
Paris, ca. 1770
Pierre Macret (active
1756–1787)
Wood marquetry, gilt bronze
H. 35 in., W. 58 in., D. 24 in.
31.9

Fig. 63
Apron mount of table in fig. 30,
by Martin Carlin

trade, the *marqueteurs*, who made certain designs to be sold to master *ébénistes*, who then inserted them into their pieces of furniture. Their existence is corroborated by the fact that similar marquetry designs appear on dissimilar pieces of furniture stamped by various different makers.

The drop-front secretary in figure sixty-five is a case in point. Similar marquetry, incorporating some of the same figures, appears on several recorded pieces. For example, the donkey at the forefront of the round medallion and the architectural ruins at the center of the drop-front (fig. 66) are also featured on the top of the Roussel table in figure fifty-six. The distinctive knotted bow in two-colored woods appears in other works attributed to or stamped by Christophe Wolff. Wolff, a German émigré, had a reputation as a fine *marqueteur*. The small medallion in the center at the top, depicting a northern seventeenth-century scene, might be an allusion to his origins. The *secretaire à abbatant* or the *secretaire en armoire* made its appearance in the 1730s.[23] It resembled a cupboard or upright cabinet with a hinged falling writing-leaf forming the central panel.

More striking is the recurrence of the same marquetry patterns on pieces of the same shape and proportions but signed by two different makers. This is the case of the tables shown in figure sixty-seven, one signed Guillaume Kemp and the other François-Gaspard Teuné. These were two cabinetmakers who specialized in simple, small- to medium-sized pieces of furniture in the

Fig. 64

Mount in center of roll-top desk
in fig. 73, depicting a putto
reclining on a truncated column

Fig. 65

DROP-FRONT
SECRETARY
(secretaire à abbatant)
Paris, ca. 1775
Attributed to Christophe Wolff
Wood marquetry, gilt bronze,
ivory, mother-of-pearl
H. 57 in., W. 40 in., D. 16 in.
31.7

transitional and neoclassical styles. It is no secret that some *ébéniste*s subcontracted their work when their shops were too busy. The same occurred with carcasses. The almost identical size and shape of these two tables suggest mass-produced carcasses by some menuisier workshops. In addition to large and important works, masters produced a number of simple—albeit perfect— pieces that could be turned out very quickly and just as quickly found a

Fig. 66

*Drop-front marquetry panel,
showing a landscape of classical
ruins framed with lattice work
and suspended from a ribbon,
detail of fig. 65*

market. André Roubo, who wrote a seminal work on French cabinetry,[24] was very critical of this practice. Many *ébénistes*, he claimed, were incapable of any but the most elementary designs. They bought ready-made carcasses from second-rate manufacturers as well as prefabricated motifs in marquetry, which they then inlaid giving little thought to the general design. Roubo admitted that the fault lay as much with the public as with the *ébénistes*. Everyone wished to own veneered furniture that was cheap and that could be supplied in short order.

The miniature *bonheur du jour* in figure sixty-eight is decorated with Chinese vessels on all sides. The work is in the manner of Charles Topino, one of the minor masters who made countless little tables and pieces such as this one decorated with Chinese objects inspired by the ornamental borders of Chinese Coromandel lacquer screens. From his diary it is known that Topino executed marquetry panels of this type for his colleagues the *marchand-ébénistes*. The function of miniature furniture is rather unclear. Although generally thought to be *chefs-d'oeuvre,* it is highly unlikely that anyone trying to graduate as a master would execute a piece on such a small scale. More plausibly, these pieces were intended to serve as children's furniture, or as an advertisement for a traveling salesman.

Functionality was a key concern of French cabinetmakers in the eighteenth century, and as letter writing was one of the favorite pastimes of the period, these makers met the demand to supply all kinds of furniture for that purpose. Flocks of servants were always in attendance to deliver a constant stream of letters. For quick letter writing, a small table would suffice. But for more serious work, all kinds of *bureaux* or desks were created. Among the smaller writing pieces is the *bonheur du jour* (fig. 69), a sort of table surmounted at the back by a superstructure fitted with doors and shelves. The name was almost certainly a marketing ploy of the *marchands-merciers*, who earned the dubious reputation of giving "bizarre names whose etymology is

Fig. 67

TWO WRITING
TABLES
Paris, ca. 1780
Wood marquetry, brass
Left: stamped G. Kemp and
J.M.E for Guillaume Kemp
(became a master in 1764)
H. 28½ in., W. 17 in.,
D. 13 in.
31.32

Fig. 67

Right: stamped F. G. Teune for
François-Gaspard Teuné
H. 27 in., W. 16 in., D. 13 in.
31.33

Fig. 68

MINIATURE
WRITING TABLE
(bonheur du jour)
Paris, ca. 1770–1775
Wood marquetry, gilt bronze
H. 19 in., W. 15 in., D. 9 in.
31.21

based solely on the caprices and the cupidity of artisans and merchants."[25] Hillwood's example, which effectively combines mahogany and teakwood, came from the famous Blumenthal collections, which made it to the auction block in several spectacular sales in 1932 and 1933.

The most monumental and ceremonial of writing pieces was the roll-top or cylinder desk. The first one was conceived by Oeben, finished by Riesener, and delivered to King Louis XV at Versailles in 1769. The form of the famous *bureau du roi* was thereafter constantly emulated.

The Roentgen desk at Hillwood (figs. 5, 70, 71, 72) goes beyond the mere functions of a roll-top desk. It served as a writing desk not only while one was seated, but also when one was standing. Furthermore, it also served as a dressing table and strongbox, judging by its numerous secret compartments and coffers. The desk is indeed a tour de force of mechanical *ébénisterie,* with more than forty secret compartments. Among the most extravagant are a mirror that when cranked up emerges from the top, and swinging lateral drawers containing candleholders fitted with green silk screens to protect against the direct heat and glare of the candles.

The desk is also extraordinary for its marquetry. Various types of wood in different shades were utilized to depict clusters of instruments suspended from ribbons. Set off against a background of sycamore, the instruments are framed with bands of tulipwood and formal motifs inlaid in mother-of-pearl. The monogram MA surmounted by a crown and topped by an orb and a cross appears at the center of the roll-top.

Is this the monogram of Marie Antoinette? Did the queen ever own the desk? The answer is probably not. However, it may have been intended for her. It was a well-known practice for Abraham Roentgen and his son David to make special pieces of furniture to present to rulers and other important people in the hope of securing commissions, as they did with Catherine the Great of Russia. When she was presented with a desk designed especially for her, she

Fig. 70

ROLL-TOP DESK

Neuwied, ca. 1770

Abraham Roentgen

(1711–1793) and David

Roentgen (1743–1807)

Wood marquetry, mother-of-

pearl, gilt bronze, steel, leather,

glass

H. 45 in.,W. 42 in., D. 25 in.

33.222

Fig. 71

View of open roll-top desk in

fig. 70

was so enthralled that orders began pouring in. The Hillwood desk has several
symbols that may allude to Marie Antoinette, namely the dolphin-shaped
bronze feet and the cipher on the roll top, which can be read as "MA."
However, the crown surmounted by the cipher would not have been
appropriate for a queen of France. One possible explanation is that work on
the desk was begun while she was dauphine of France, but was completed only
after she had become queen (1774) and was thus unquestionably inappropriate

for her. It would also have been rather old-fashioned for someone known to be a follower of the latest trends. Alternatively, it could have been made for a German prince or elector, for whom such a crown would have been acceptable and who was an important client of the Roentgens.

Roentgen, as a foreign cabinetmaker, was obliged to join the guild of *ébénistes* and to sell his works through a specified *dépôt* in Paris.

Of more modest proportions and of simpler execution is the roll-top desk signed by Conrad Mauter (fig. 73). Gilt-bronze mounts form a visually pleasing contrast with the rich mahogany color. The singularly special bronze plaque of a putto reclining on rocky ground, which is mounted on the roll-top, deserves special notice (fig. 64). Also special are the female allegorical figures with plumed helmets that terminate in tapering acanthus leaves. The desk stands as one of this cabinetmaker's most ambitious productions. His other work consisted largely of simple mahogany pieces of austere lines. Mauter was one of the many cabinetmakers of German descent working in Paris. In 1782 he became cabinetmaker to the comte d'Artois, brother of Louis XVI. The gilt-bronze helmeted figures and the prominent sprays of laurel leaves suggest that the desk was intended for someone with a distinguished military career or for a member of the royal family holding an honorary military rank, perhaps for d'Artois himself (fig. 74).

Mauter's desk is a good example of the taste for simple veneers, one of the English fashions that the French adopted with fervor at a time when Anglomania swept the country. The Marquis de Marigny, Mme. Pompadour's brother and a sort of minister of culture, ordered his *ébéniste* Pierre Garnier to craft several pieces of furniture with simple mahogany veneers. Mahogany, a

Fig. 73
ROLL-TOP DESK
(bureau à cylindre)
Paris, ca. 1780
Conrad Mauter (1742–1810)
Mahogany, gilt bronze, leather,
H.48 in.,W. 59 in., D. 28 in.
31.2

Fig. 74
Detail of fig. 73
(Also illustrated on pages 2–3)

Fig. 75
TALL CABINET
Paris, ca. 1780–1790
Mahogany, gilt bronze
H. 47½ in., W. 24¾ in.,
D. 16¾ in.
31.5

hard, durable wood with a close grain, was ideal for cabinetmaking. A French visitor to England noted: "the English are so much given to the use of mahogany; not only are their tables generally made of it, but also their doors and seats and the handrails of their staircases. Yet it is just as dear in England as it is in France. . . . In any event, their tables are made of most beautiful wood and always have a brilliant polish like that of the finest glass."[26] But the treatment mahogany received in England is totally different from the one it received in France. Because of the English hegemony in the Caribbean and in the East Indies, where mahogany was grown, the English used solid planks of the wood, which they carved with high-relief ornamentation. The loss of France's colonial power in the East and West Indies limited supplies of the wood. Mahogany was too precious to use in the solid, and therefore was used as a veneer, relying on the decorative aspects of its figure and grain.[27]

The upright cabinet in figure seventy-five sports the most exquisite mahogany surfaces of a rich, deep, reddish-brown color, with a figuring resembling flames. Of rather unusual proportions, and of severe neoclassical ornamentation, the cabinet conceals drawers and shelves behind doors. Unsigned mahogany furniture with these types of mounts has been alternatively attributed to J.-H. Riesener, B. Molitor, G. Benneman, and E. Levasseur.

Identical gilt-bronze key escutcheons can be found on several pieces signed by Riesener.

The austerity of the furniture of the late 1780s mirrors the political climate of Paris on the eve of the Revolution. The economic crisis and declining income among the urban working class affected journeymen and unprivileged workers in particular. They mobilized as the *san-culottes,*[28] from whom the urban revolutionaries drew much of their support. As for the role of the *menuisiers* and *ébénistes* of Paris in the Revolution, the fact that most of the mob that stormed the Bastille on the 14th of July was made up of craftsmen of the Faubourg Saint-Antoine speaks for itself. Among these craftsmen were furniture makers, especially foreign ones. Salverte lists around sixty foreigners among those who took the Bastille, including a host of Germans from "all the Germanies"—Prussia, Austria, Bavaria, and Saxony.[29]

But not all *menuisiers* and *ébénistes* supported the revolution. The older masters either retired or continued working, faithful to the traditional system. Some who had gained a major reputation were respected and spared the persecution of the Revolution. Even so, their livelihoods were affected. Jean-Henri Riesener was ruined. The lack of new commissions along with the unpaid bills of the Crown and the nobles who fled the country, left Riesener in a desperate financial state. So when the Convention put the property of the Crown up for sale, Riesener took the risky step of buying his own works in the hope of reselling them when the disturbance had passed. But in January 1794, at the height of the Terror, he was forced to sell everything he had in his workshop. Despite the turbulent times, Riesener continued working. However, the new aesthetic doctrines had discredited the art of the time of Louis XVI, and everyone knew Riesener had been the king's official *ébéniste*.

Georges Jacob chose a very different course of action during the Revolution, exploiting the new political situation to the full. Jacob was a supporter of the cause. As a result, Jacob's business prospered under the

Revolution. Thanks to the protection of his friend and admirer, the painter Jacques-Louis David, he was spared the persecutions of the Terror. Where he had previously supplied Marie Antoinette, he now supplied the Revolution: the furniture of the house of session of the Convention, in the Tuileries, was made by him. Soon after the Revolution, he retired from his craft. His two sons inherited his industrial-scale workshop and named it Jacob Frères. The Jacob dynasty subsequently provided furniture to Napoleon, his family, and his court.

Regardless of the paths that each furniture maker took, the panorama at the end of the Revolution had changed. The golden age of furniture making had come to an end.

Notes

Fig. 76
Detail of fig. 9

1. "Hillwood Becoming a Museum," *Antique Monthly*, October 1971, p. 21.

2. The preparatory volumes are kept with Hillwood's curatorial papers.

3. Letter in curatorial file 31.27, n.d.

4. Letter in curatorial file 31.11, dated January 14, 1963.

5. "*Monuments érigés en France à la gloire de Louis XV,*" "*C'est l'art de la distribution des bâtiments; rien ne nous a tant fait honneur que cette invention. Avant ce temps, on donnait tout à l'extérieur et à la magnificence. A l'exemple des bâtiments antiques et de tous ceux de l'Italie que l'on prenait pour modèles, les intérieures étaient vastes et sans aucune commodité. C'étaient des salons à double étage, des spacieuses salles de compagnie, des salles de festins immenses, des galeries à perte de vue, des escaliers d'une grandeur extraordinaire; toutes ces pièces étaient placées sans dégagement, au bout les unes des autres On était logé uniquement pour réprésenter, et l'on ignorait l'art de se loger commodément et pour soi. . . .*" J. Feray, *Architecture intérieure et décoration en France des origines à nos jours* (Paris, 1977), p. 193.

6. "*Une chambre ne doit pas ressembler à un magasin de marchand,*" ibid., p. 240.

7. Bruno Pons, *French Period Rooms* (Paris, 1995), p. 150.

8. Gilles Demarteau l'aîné, *Plusieurs Trophées Déssinées et Gravés par Demarteau l'aîné. . . .* Paris [n.d.].

9. The painting entitled "*Ruines à la Pyramide*" is in the Musée des Beaux Arts in Valence, France. The painting was engraved by P. F. Tardieu, who must have served as the source for the *marqueteur*.

10. "*Tous les six ans, on change son ameublement. Les meubles sont devenus les plus grands objets de luxe et de dépense.*" Quoted from J. Feray, *Architecture*, p. 308. From Louis Sébastien Mercier, *Tableau de Paris* (Amsterdam, 1781).

11. For a discussion on the subject, see L. Auslander, *Taste and Power: Furnishing Modern France* (Berkeley–London, 1996), pp. 67–68.

12. J. F. Blondel, *De la distribution des maisons de plaisance et de la décoration des édifices en général 1737–38,* in J. Mariette's monumental *Architecture française, 1727,* whose third volume contains a series of plates illustrating the most modern decorations.

13. "*Par leur experience et leur capacité, ont contribue à rendre nos demeures des séjours enchantés, dignes de l'opulence de la plupart de nos concitoyens et de l'admiration des nations non prévenues*," J. F. Blondel, *Discours de la nécessité de l'étude de l'architecture* (Paris, 1752). Quoted from J. Feray, *Architecture intérieure et décoration en France* (Paris, 1997), p. 188.

14. Much of Pineau's mural decoration was published; no fewer than 60 plates appeared in the 4th volume of Jean Mariette's *Architecture française*. Blondel's *De la distribution des maisons de plaisance et de la décoration des édifices en général, 1737–38* is devoted to the style for which Pineau is celebrated.

15. "*Quand une maison est bâtie, rien n'est fait encore; on n'est pas au quart de la dépense: arrivent le menuisier, le tapissier, le peintre, le doreur, le sculpteur, l'ébéniste. . . . L'aménagement de l'hôtel occupe trois fois plus de temps que la construction de l'hôtel*," Louis Sébastien Mercier, *Tableau de Paris* (Amsterdam, 1782–88), p. 166.

16. See Maria Isabel Pereira Coutinho, *Eighteenth-Century French Furniture: The Calouste Gulbenkian Museum* (Lisbon, 1999), pp. 73–74.

17. See *Masterpieces from Versailles: Three Centuries of French Portraiture* (Washington D.C., 1983), no. 21.

18. Bill Pallot, *The Art of the Chair in Eighteenth-century France* (Paris, 1989), p. 110.

19. See Svend Eriksen, *Early Neoclassicism in France* (London, 1974), p. 86 and fig. 389, showing a detail of Badouin's engraving entitled "*Le Lever.*"

20. "*Aujourd'hui, les moeurs sont plus unies, les canapés et les chaises longues sont employés par les dames, sans causer d'embarras dans la société*," J. Feray, 1997, p. 255.

21. The *Garde-Meuble* was a department responsible for royal commissions of furnishings, their conservation, distribution, and inventory.

22. J. Bantam, ed., *Encyclopedia of Interior Design* (London, 1997), vol. 1, p. 303.

23. Sir Geoffrey de Bellaigue, in his catalogue *The James A. de Rothschild Collection at Waddesdon Manor* (Fribourg, 1974), cat. no. 102, pp. 498–500, discusses the attribution of a group of pieces to this master. This group includes a table in the Rothschild collection in Waddesdon Manor, Buckinghamshire; a table in the Jones collection at the Victoria & Albert Museum, London; and a table in the Louvre, Paris.

24. André Jacob Roubo, *L'art du menuisier* (Paris, 1769–1775).

25. "*Noms bizarres qui n'ont d'autre étymologie que le caprice ou la cupidité des ouvriers et des marchands.*" Quoted from Charles Oulmont, *La Vie au dix-huitième siècle: La Maison* (Paris, 1929), p. 60.

26. J. Marchand, ed. (1933), *Mélanges sur l'Angleterre of François de la Rochefoucauld*, 1734. Quoted from Clive Edwards, *Encyclopedia* (Cambridge, 2000), p. 130.

27. For more information on the subject of availability of woods, read Ulrich Leben et al., eds., *Bernard Molitor, 1755–1833* (Luxembourg, 1995) and, in particular, pp. 58–62.

28. *Sans-culottes* was the term originally given to the ill-clad and ill-equipped volunteers of the Revolutionary army in the early stages of the French Revolution. Their distinctive costume was the *pantalon*, in place of the *culottes* worn by the upper classes.

29. Comte de Salverte, *Les Ebénistes du XVIIIe siècle: Leurs oeuvres et leurs marques* (Paris, 1953), p. XIX.

Selected Bibliography

Auslander, Leora. *Taste and Power: Furnishing Modern France* (Berkeley, Calif.: University of California Press, 1996)

Bellaigue, Geoffrey de. *The James A. de Rothschild Collection at Waddesdon Manor: Furniture, Clocks and Gilt Bronzes.* 2 vols. (Fribourg: Office du Livre, 1974)

Dell, Theodore. *The Frick Collection: An Illustrated Catalogue*, vols. 5 and 6, *Furniture and Gilt Bronzes* (Princeton, N.J.: Princeton University Press, 1992)

Eriksen, Svend. *Early Neoclassicism in France* (London: Faber & Faber, 1974)

Feray, Jean. *Architecture intérieure et décoration en France, des origines à 1875* (Paris: Berger-Levrault, 1988)

Hughes, Peter. *The Wallace Collection: Catalogue of Furniture* (London: The Trustees of the Wallace Collections, 1996)

Kjellberg, Pierre. *Le Mobilier français du XVIIIe siècle: Dictionnaire des ébénistes et des menuisiers* (Paris: Editions de l'amateur, 1989)

Odom, Anne and Liana Paredes Arend. *A Taste for Splendor: Russian Imperial and European Treasures from the Hillwood Museum* (Alexandria, Va.: Art Services International, 1998)

Pallot, Bill G. B. *The Art of the Chair in Eighteenth-century France* (Paris: ACR-Gismondi, 1989)

Pereira Coutinho, Maria Isabel. *Eighteenth-century French Furniture* (Lisbon: Calouste Gulbenkian Museum, 1999)

Pons, Bruno. *French Period Rooms, 1650–1800* (Dijon: Editions Faton, 1995)

Pradère, Alexandre. *French Furniture Makers: The Art of the Ebéniste from Louis XIV to the Revolution* (Malibu, Calif.: The J. Paul Getty Museum, 1989)

Verlet, Pierre. *French Royal Furniture* (New York: Clarkson N. Potter, 1963)

Whitehead, John. *The French Interior in the Eighteenth Century* (London: L. King, 1992)

Library of Congress Cataloging-in-Publication Data
Arend, Liana Paredes, 1961-
    French Furniture from the Collection of Hillwood Museum & Gardens /
Liana Paredes Arend ; curator of western European art.
        p. cm.
    ISBN 1-931485-03-8 (Hardcover) — ISBN 1-931485-04-6 (Softcover)
    1. Furniture–France–History–18th century. 2. Furniture–Washington (D.C.) 3. Hillwood
Museum and Gardens. I. Hillwood Museum and Gardens. II. Title.
    NK2548 .A74 2003
    749.24'09'033–dc21

                                                                    2002011966

Photographer: EDWARD OWEN
Editor: GRACE MORSBERGER
Designer: POLLY FRANCHINI
Printer: SCHNEIDEREITH AND SONS

Cover: detail of figure 49, page 81
Frontispiece: detail of figure 49, page 81
Pages 2–3: detail of figure 73, page 110
Page 4: detail of figure 72, page 108